SONGS FOR SIGHT-SINGIN VOLUME 2

Junior High School — Tenor-Bass

Compiled by
Mary Henry and Marilyn Jones

Consulting Editor
Dr. Ruth Whitlock

Director of Music Education Studies
Texas Christian University

SOUTHERN MUSIC COMPANY
Publishing Division

B518

Table of Contents

B518

Preface

The anthologies SONGS FOR SIGHT-SINGING and SONGS FOR SIGHT-SINGING Volume 2 provide a collection of literature for use in the choral classroom. Each selection was composed according to criteria designed by Texas secondary choral directors and commissioned by the University of Texas Interscholastic League for use in its annual sight singing contest. These graded materials were created specifically for young musicians by recognized composers and comprise a valuable resource as they contain many of the problems encountered in sight singing. This collection can be used effectively as a supplement to the daily instructional sight singing program after an approved system of pitch reference (movable "do", fixed "do" or numbers) and a rhythm system are established within the choral curriculum

OUR FEARFUL TRIP IS DONE

WALT WHITMAN

BOBBY L. SILTMAN

GALLANT MEN

Words and Music by
BOBBY L. SILTMAN

Through-out the a - ges there have been gal - lant men.

Brave, no - ble lea - ders whose cou - rage now as then.

These men of cour - age, their voi - ces ring forth clear.

Hear now the mes - sage of free - dom for all men.

"Give me lib - er - ty, or give me death."

"Give me lib-er-ty, or give me death." I re-gret that I've but one life to give. On-ly one life to give, on-ly one life for my coun-try. Through-out the a-ges there have been gal-lant men. Brave, no-ble lea-ders whose cou-rage now as then. Give us the cou-rage to be as no-ble men, To-day and to-mor-row we will be gal-lant men.

RISE UP! HEAR THE BELLS

WALT WHITMAN

BOBBY L. SILTMAN

B518

Star of the East
TB

REGINALD HEBER

EMILY CROCKER

B518

LEONARD WAGGONER

Our Lady

BOBBY L. SILTMAN

Love - ly la - dy of our land, Light of free - dom in her hand

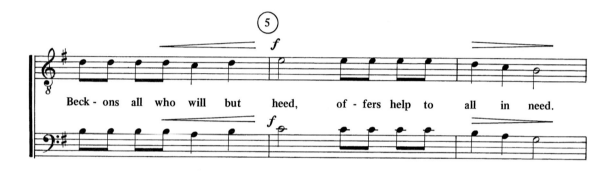

Beck - ons all who will but heed, of - fers help to all in need.

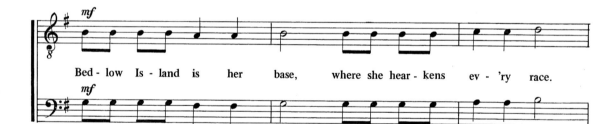

Bed - low Is - land is her base, where she hear - kens ev - 'ry race.

Turned a - way be - cause of pride, Then her tears she can - not hide.

Christmas Eve

AUTHOR UNKNOWN

BOB SILTMAN

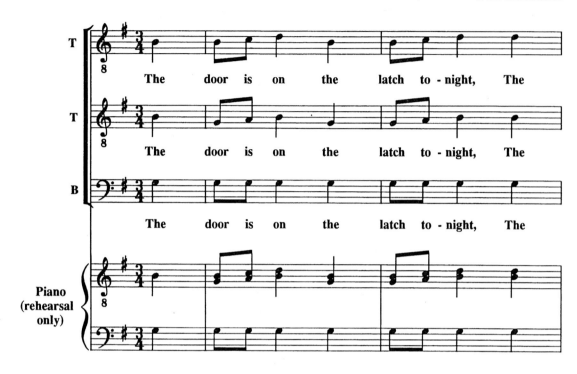

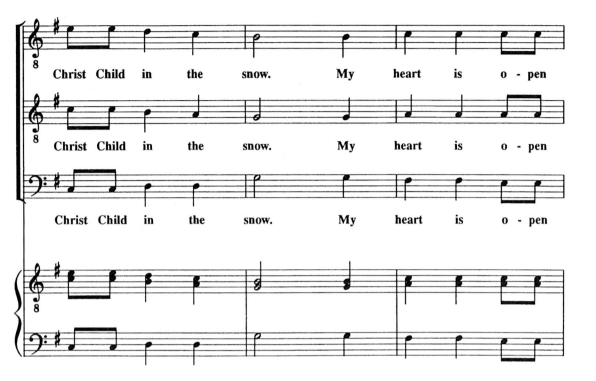

Christ Child in the snow. My heart is o - pen

Christ Child in the snow. My heart is o - pen

Christ Child in the snow. My heart is o - pen

wide to - night for stran - ger, kith or kin; I would not bar a

wide to - night for stran - ger, kith or kin; I would not bar a

wide to - night for stran - ger, kith or kin; I would not bar a

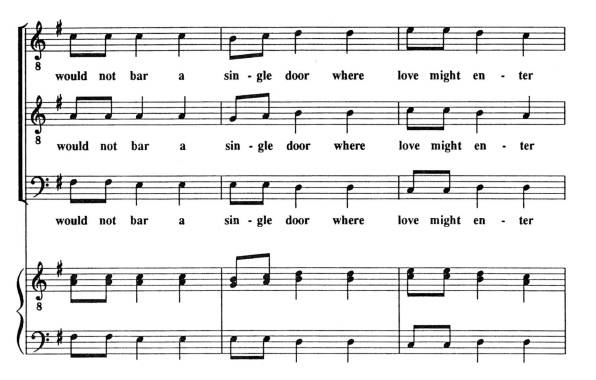

would not bar a sin - gle door where love might en - ter

would not bar a sin - gle door where love might en - ter

would not bar a sin - gle door where love might en - ter

25

in, Where love might en - ter in. ____

in, Where love might en - ter in. ____

in, Where love might en - ter in. ____

25

I Will Lift My Eyes

Text from **PSALM 121**

SHARI RILEY

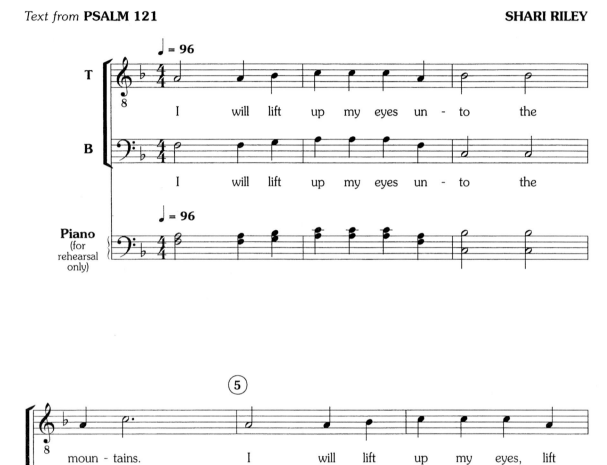

B518

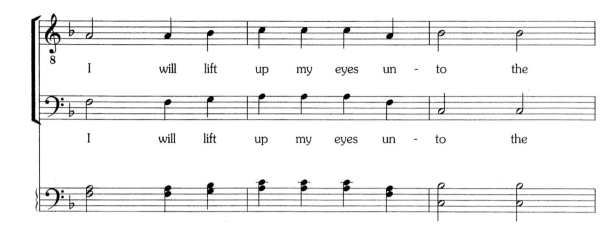

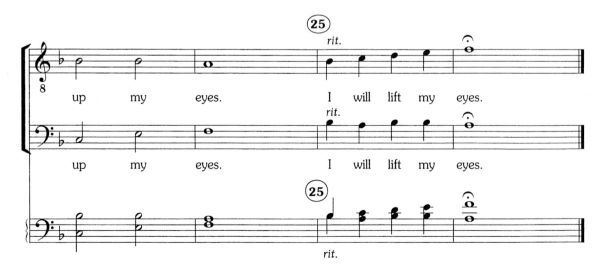

LIVE IN PEACE

Words and Music by
BOBBY L. SILTMAN

B518

nev - er know the hate, the fear of war. But

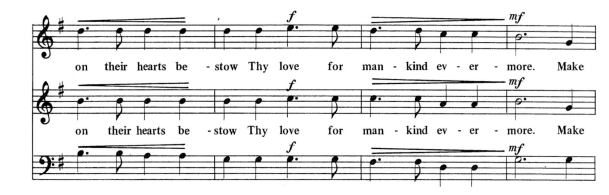

on their hearts be - stow Thy love for man - kind ev - er - more. Make

men of war lay down their arms, their guns be ev - er still, Oh

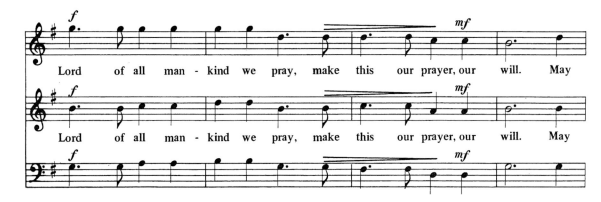

Lord of all man - kind we pray, make this our prayer, our will. May

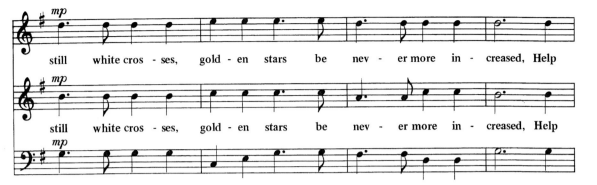

still white cros - ses, gold - en stars be nev - er more in - creased, Help

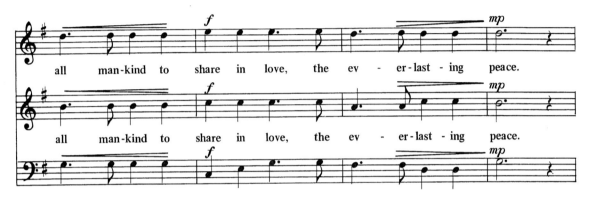

all man-kind to share in love, the ev - er-last - ing peace.

Hear our plea, our heart - felt cry, may cru - el ha - tred cease. Help

us to show our fel - low man, that we must live in peace.

B518

Celebrate Freedom

LEONARD WAGGONER

BOBBY L. SILTMAN

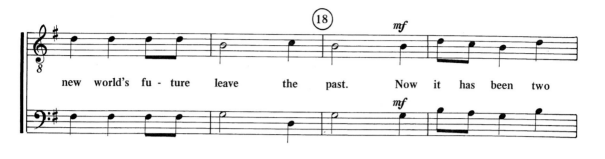

new world's fu - ture   leave   the   past.   Now   it   has   been   two

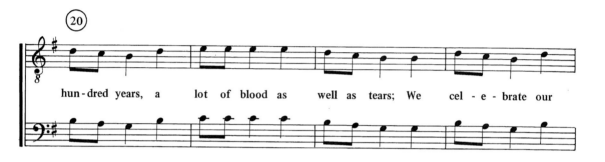

hun - dred years, a   lot of blood as   well as tears;   We   cel - e - brate our

free - doms strong. It's   on   to vic - t'ry   we   be - long. We   cel - e - brate our

free - doms strong. It's   on   to vic - t'ry   we   be - long.

The Millstream

Words and Music by
PATTI DEWITT

I Walk by the Sea

Words & Music by
PATTI DEWITT

B518

THE AIRBORNE

Words & Music by
RAE MOSES

Epitaph

Words by
ROBERT LOUIS STEVENSON

Music by
LOU WILLIAMS-WIMBERLY

Home is the sail - or, home from the sea, And the hun - ter

Home is the sail - or, home from the sea, And the hun - ter

Home is the sail - or, home from the sea, And the hun - ter

home from the hill. Home where I longed to — be.

home from the hill. Home where I longed to — be.

home from the hill. Home where I longed to — be.

THE MUSTANG

Words and Music by
PATTI DEWITT

Out on the prai - rie, wild and free, roams a colt with gol - den mane, Young and bold and full of glee, Prince of the grand and

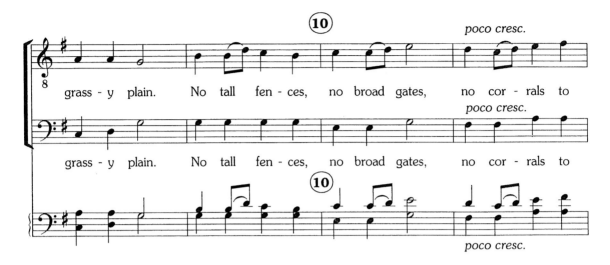

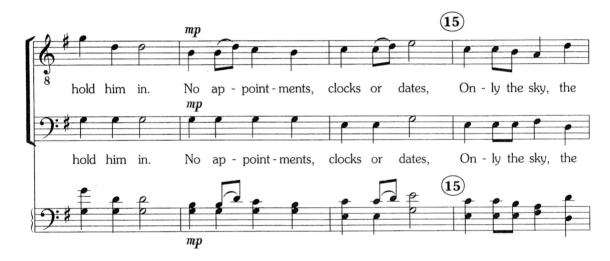

B518

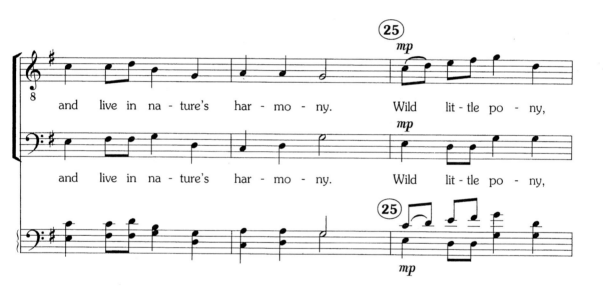

BALLOONS

Words & Music by
PATTI DEWITT

B518

42

God Bless Our Country

Words and Music by
SHARI RILEY

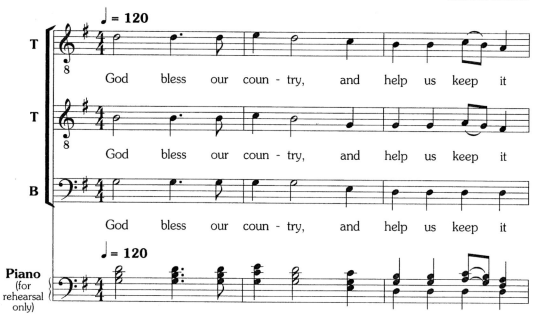

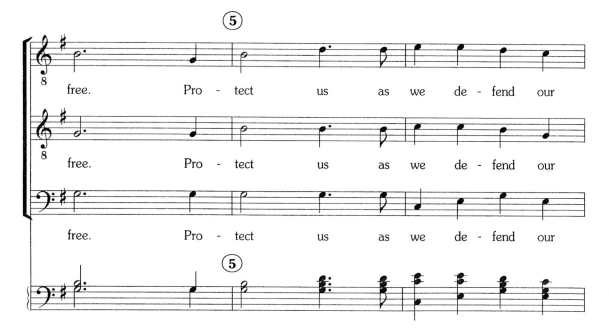

B518

li - ber - ty with gui - dance from Your hand.

li - ber - ty with gui - dance from Your hand.

li - ber - ty with gui - dance from Your hand.

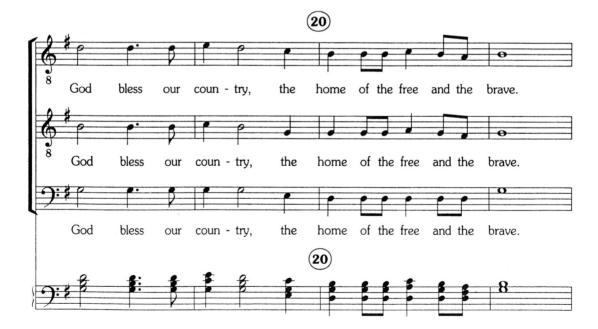

God bless our coun - try, the home of the free and the brave.

God bless our coun - try, the home of the free and the brave.

God bless our coun - try, the home of the free and the brave.

THE PRIZE WE SOUGHT IS WON

WALT WHITMAN

BOBBY L. SILTMAN

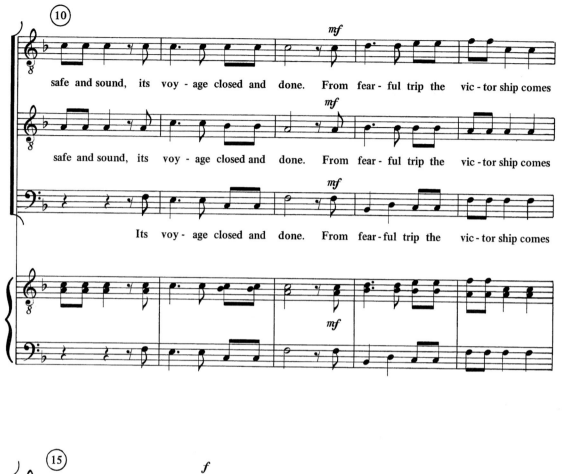

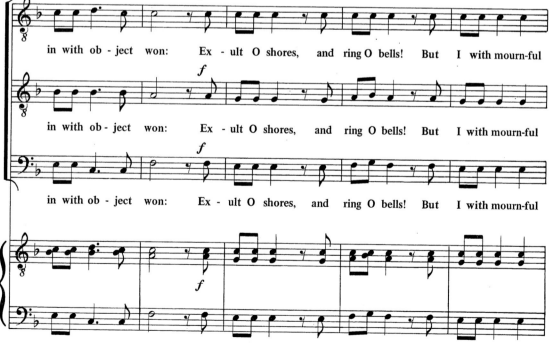

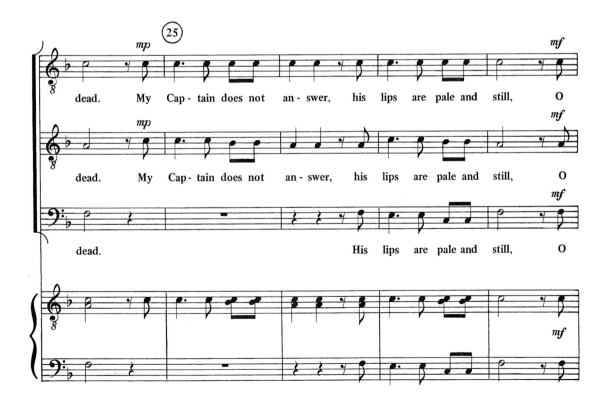

Let Freedom Ring

TBB

LEONARD WAGGONER

BOBBY L. SILTMAN

B518

B518

54

B518

Southern Music
SONGS FOR SIGHT SINGING COLLECTIONS

SONGS FOR SIGHT SINGING *provides a collection of literature for use in the choral classroom. Each selection was composed according to the criteria designed by Texas choral directors and commissioned by the Texas University Interscholastic League for use in its annual sight singing contest. These graded materials were created specifically for young musicians by recognized composers and comprise a valuable resource as they contain many of the problems encountered in sight singing. This collection can be used effectively as a supplement to the daily instructional sight singing program after an approved system (movable "do", fixed "do" or numbers) and a rhythm system are established within the choral curriculum.*

VOLUME 1
edited by Mary Henry, Marilyn Jones and Ruth Whitlock
B370 Songs for Sight Singing Vol. 1: HIGH SCHOOL/ SA
B371 Songs for Sight Singing Vol. 1: HIGH SCHOOL/ TB
B372 Songs for Sight Singing Vol. 1: HIGH SCHOOL/ SATB
B373 Songs for Sight Singing Vol. 1: JUNIOR HIGH/ SA
B374 Songs for Sight Singing Vol. 1: JUNIOR HIGH/ TB
B375 Songs for Sight Singing Vol. 1: JUNIOR HIGH/ SATB
B376 Songs for Sight Singing Vol. 1: JUNIOR HIGH - HIGH SCHOOL/ SAB

VOLUME 2
edited by Mary Henry, Marilyn Jones and Ruth Whitlock
B514 Songs for Sight Singing Vol. 2: HIGH SCHOOL/ SA
B515 Songs for Sight Singing Vol. 2: HIGH SCHOOL/ TB
B516 Songs for Sight Singing Vol. 2: HIGH SCHOOL/ SATB
B517 Songs for Sight Singing Vol. 2: JUNIOR HIGH/ SA
B518 Songs for Sight Singing Vol. 2: JUNIOR HIGH/ TB
B519 Songs for Sight Singing Vol. 2: JUNIOR HIGH/ SATB
B520 Songs for Sight Singing Vol. 2: JUNIOR HIGH - HIGH SCHOOL/ SAB

VOLUME 3
edited by Vivian Munn and Renee Higgins
B557 Songs for Sight Singing Vol. 3: HIGH SCHOOL/ SATB
B558 Songs for Sight Singing Vol. 3: HIGH SCHOOL/ SA
B559 Songs for Sight Singing Vol. 3: HIGH SCHOOL/ TB
B560 Songs for Sight Singing Vol. 3: JUNIOR HIGH - HIGH SCHOOL/ SAB
B561 Songs for Sight Singing Vol. 3: JUNIOR HIGH/ SATB
B562 Songs for Sight Singing Vol. 3: JUNIOR HIGH/ SA
B563 Songs for Sight Singing Vol. 3: JUNIOR HIGH/ TB